# A Drug Ad~~~ St

**How to End Drug Addiction and Get Life Back On Track**

## By: Rachel Chloe Sanchez

## 9781681275178

# PUBLISHERS NOTES

## Disclaimer – Speedy Publishing LLC

Speedy Publishing LLC

40 E Main Street, Newark, Delaware, 19711

Contact Us: 1-888-248-4521

Website: http://www.speedypublishing.co

REPRINTED Paperback Edition: 9781681275178:

Manufactured in the United States of America

# DEDICATION

This book is dedicated to my darling Sebastian. Son, mommy will be waiting for you when you come back home.

# TABLE OF CONTENTS

# CHAPTER 1- WHY ARE DRUGS ADDICTIVE?

Drugs are chemicals, which can change the way bodies work. If you have ever been sick and take medicine, you already have an idea about the different types of drugs. Medicines are drugs that doctors provide to those who are sick. But, did you know that even medicines can be dangerous if they are not taken carefully. There are some kinds of drugs that are dangerous all the time. These are not given by physicians or doctors. Cigarettes and alcohol are included in these kinds of drugs. Even if people can purchase these legally at stores, these can be dangerous. Illegal drugs are also harmful and these may include marijuana, LSD, heroin, ecstasy, and cocaine.

**Types of Drugs**

You have probably heard that drugs can be bad for you. But, why are they bad? And what does that mean? Below are the different kinds of drugs you should be aware of for you to know their effects and impacts to your life:

## Medicines – The Legal Drugs

If you are sick and you take medicine to feel better, you already know this kind of drugs. Medicines are considered as legal drugs. This just means that doctors are allowed to give medicines for patients. Store may also sell them and individuals are allowed to purchase them. However, it is not safe or legal for people to take medicines in any way they like or buy them from those who are selling these in an illegal manner.

## Alcohol and Cigarettes

Alcohol and cigarettes are other kinds of legal drugs. In most countries, people who are 18 years old and above can purchase cigarettes and those who are 21 years old and above could purchase alcohol. However, excessive drinking and smoking aren't healthy for adults and are prohibited to kids.

## Illegal Drugs

When individuals talk about drug problems, they typically mean abusing illegal or legal drugs including ecstasy, cocaine, marijuana, crystal meth, heroin, and LSD. Generally, marijuana is an illegal. But, due to its health benefits, some states let doctors recommend it to adults for particular illnesses.

## Illegal Drugs Spell Danger

Illegal drugs are not good for everyone. They are bad for teens and kids whose bodies are still growing. Illegal drugs could damage one's heart, brain, and some organs. For instance, cocaine can cause heart attack even in a teen or a kid.

While using such drugs, individuals are also less able to perform well in school, sports, and several activities. It is frequently harder to think clearly and create wise decisions. People may do dangerous or dumb things, which could hurt themselves or some people when using drugs.

**Reasons for Illegal Drug Use**

Sometimes, teens and kids try using drugs to fit in a group of peers. There are cases that they are bored or curious. Someone could also use illegal drugs for several reasons, but in most cases, they take these for helping persons escape from reality. Drugs might make someone feel better and forget about their problems temporarily. But, this escape could last only until drugs wear off.

Drugs do not solve problems. Using drugs could cause other problems aside from the problems you have. Somebody who is using these could become addicted. This just means that the body of the person may become so accustomed to have this drug that he or she can't do well without this.

Once you are addicted to these drugs, it is tough to stop taking them. Stopping may cause withdrawal symptoms including sweating, tremors,

**Commonly Used Illegal Drugs**

What drugs are commonly abused?

● Intoxicants/Alcohol

● Cannabis/Marijuana

● Methaqualone /Mandrax

- Diacetylmorphine/Heroin

- Flunitrazepan/Rohypnol

- Methylenedioxymethamphetamine/Ecstasy

- O-methylmorphine /Codeine

- Antianxiety Agents

- Lysergic acid diethylamide/LSD

- Metamfetamine /Crystal methamphetamine (Meth)

- Amphetamine /Speed

- Benzoylmethylecgonine/Cocaine

- Appetite suppressants

- Cough mixture

- Inhalants

- Prescription pain or sleeping medicine

**The Disadvantages of Drug Use**

There are numerous things that can happen from drug addiction and none of them are really positive. The negative outcomes of an addiction could be listed for days, so instead of rambling on I will give you an example of a few things that will almost certainly happen.

**Loss of Relationships:**

Everyone has their breaking point. This means that no matter how much someone may love someone else, they get to a certain point where they can no longer take the stress or the fear and are forced to part ways. This will likely fuel the addiction and make problems even worse. In fact, many of these situations end in suicide or other terrible outcomes.

**Jail:**

As a drug addict, it will not be very long until you are arrested. The law enforcement agencies are getting tired of the abundance of drugs and are starting to give out much more stiff penalties, even to first time offenders. Having drug charges on your record will surely add complication to your financial situation since getting a good job would be very difficult.

**STDs:**

Some drug use may lead to STDs. Especially drugs that are injected. The rate of people with HIV and Hepatitis C in the drug community is outrageous. Many addicts begin to not care about hygiene and safety and will begin sharing needles and having unprotected sex with people they normally wouldn't.

**Death:**

An addiction will eventually lead to death. It does not matter how much a person thinks that they are in control and can stop at any time, they are delusional! Abusing drugs slowly kills addicts as well as damages the health of those who care for them due to the high stress of the situation. You must begin recovery!

# CHAPTER 2- SIGNS AND SYMPTOMS OF DRUG USE

If someone is using such drugs, you will notice changes in how person acts or looks. Below are some of the signs. Some who use drugs could:

• Lose interest in going to school

• Hang out with kids who are also using drugs

• Become negative, worried, cranky or moody all the time

• Want to be alone all the time

• Can't concentrate

- Sleep every time especially during class

- Always gets fights

- Gain or lose weight

- Have runny nose all the time

- Cough a lot

- Have puffy or red eyes

**What Can You Do?**

If you think your kid is using drugs, the best thing you should do is to have some talk about drugs. Drug talks are essential most particularly if your kid is always curious about drugs and want to know if these are really risky or not.

When having a drug talk, you should understand about drugs and why these are dangerous. Being familiar with some terms like the following can be helpful:

- Addiction – Someone is experiencing addiction if she or he becomes dependent on drugs all the time.

- Depressant – Depressants are drugs that slow a person down. Physicians prescribe depressants in helping people be less anxious, angry or tense. Depressants can also relax muscles and make anyone feel less stressed out or sleepy. Several individuals can also use such drugs in an illegal manner to slow themselves down as well as help bring on sleep particularly after using different types of stimulants.

- Stimulant – Stimulants speed up the brain and body. Some of these are cocaine and methamphetamines. These have opposite of depressants. Typically, stimulants can make someone feel energized and high. When effects of stimulants wear off, a person will feel sick or tired.

- Narcotic – Narcotics dull the senses of the body and relieves pain. These may cause someone to fall into the stupor, sleep, slip into coma, and have convulsions. Particular narcotics like codeine are legal if provided by doctors in treating pain. Heroin is also an illegal narcotic as this has harmful side effects and can be very addictive.

- Hallucinogen – Hallucinogens are a drug like LSD, which changes the mood of the person and makes her or him hear or see things that are not really there or think of some strange things.

- High – This is the feeling, which drug users like to acquire when taking drugs. There are numerous kinds of highs like a spacey feeling or very happy, which someone has special powers like ability to see the future or fly.

- Inhalant – Like gasoline or glue, once sniffed could provide users an immediate rush. Inhalants generate a quick feeling of getting drunk, which can be followed by staggering, confusion, sleepiness, and dizziness.

**What is Drug Dependency?**

A substance abuse issue is commonly diagnosed when the substance abuser seeks help for this issue, or an interested family member encourages an appointment with a general doctor, drug counselor or psychologist. If you choose to look for help, you are

*Rachel Chloe Sanchez*

able to expect to be asked a couple of questions concerning your substance use and any troubles you might be going through.

You might likewise be asked if you have ever tried to, or sensed that you ought to quit or cut back, if you experience any shame or feel that you might have a problem, or if you have ever taken substances as a way of "grappling" with life issues.

A few people who have tried out substances or use them often will recognize when infrequent drug use gets to be drug abuse and dependency. Self-denial all the same, is really powerful and might blind a lot of individuals to the truth that substances are becoming an issue. Substance abuse and dependency may be recognized by the accompanying signs:

• Sensing that you have to have the drug on a steady basis

• Seeing to it that you have a ceaseless supply of the substance

• Acting in uncharacteristic ways in order to use, like theft of money, lying to family members, or turning aggressive when something stands between you and your succeeding drug taking time

• Feeling lost when trying to deal with life's issues and stressors without the „help" from your substance of choice

• Repeatedly bombing attempts at terminating your drug use

• Developing of tolerance toward the substance

• Placing yourself and/or other people in danger when under the influence, like driving while inebriated, or taking part in other hazardous behaviors, including unguarded sex

- Decline in quality in relationships, work performance or financial position

- Frictions with authority, the police or other legal issues

- Excusing use – "everybody does it", "require it to relax", "it's only sleeping pills/marijuana"

The questions that appear to arise time and time again when viewing drug abuse are: "Why may a few individuals take drugs without ever getting addicted to or dependent upon them?", "How come a few individuals quit chronic drug use, but other people go forward with a lifelong pattern of substance abuse and addiction in spite of a lot of failed attempts to quit?" These queries have been the motivation for a great deal of research.

**The Evolution of Drug Addiction**

Genetic elements - drug abuse as a whole appears to run in families and studies have resolved that dependency has a genetic element. While environmental components influence whether somebody uses substances misuse and dependency might be for the most part influenced by genetics.

Pitiful coping and self-medication – a lot of individuals enter the world of substance abuse as a means of running away from objectionable feelings like depressive disorder, stress or anxiousness and it gets to be a way to cope with stress. Other people use substances as a sort of self-medication. For instance, an individual enduring social anxiety might take drugs in order to become less subdued and more fearless of social situations.

Highs - Different substances have different psychological results and produce different mood states. For instance cannabis is frequently taken as a relaxant, where cocaine is a stimulant drug and is commonly taken to bring on a state of vigor and euphoria. These senses are enjoyable and serve as positive reward - individuals carry on to take substances to recapture this enjoyable high.

Lows - Differently, what climbs up must fall. There comes a point in substance addiction where it takes more and more to achieve these enjoyable highs and so more substances are ingested. The more drugs that are ingested, the more difficult the "fall" will be. A few individuals get into deeply painful and dejected states and ingesting a lot of drugs is often seen as the only way to alleviate these objectionable feelings.

Societal and cultural components – a lot of youngsters are exposed to the theme of substances at an early age by their parents, siblings, peers and the mass medium. Youngsters that have had substance misusing parents are more likely to utilize drugs themselves as are those whose societal peer group promotes the theme of drugs. Likewise, cultural values place different accent on the perceptual experience of substances.

# CHAPTER 3- TREATMENTS CUSTOMIZED BASED ON ADDICTIVE SUBSTANCE

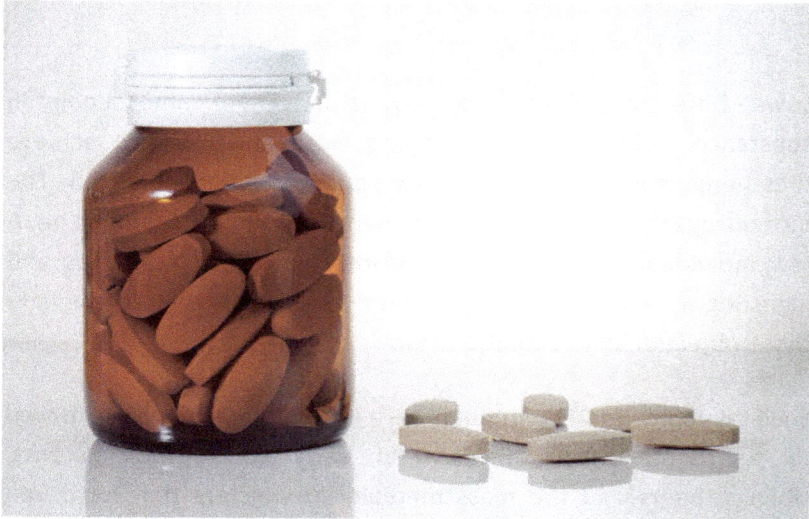

• **Treatment of Opiate Drug User**

Opiate drug users oftentimes get treatment in methadone plans, where behavioral/psychosocial therapies are blended with a medicine to control heroin use. Their additional illicit drug utilization, particularly cocaine, is frequently a primary objective of behavioral interventions.

Enquiry has now shown that substance abuse counseling with abstinence inducement processes and access to psychosocial services is an active component in the treatment procedure; and that more services brought about better results.

Among patients in a methadone upkeep sample, 90 - 100% who got psychosocial services and incentive processes were abstinent from heroin and cocaine for as long as eight weeks; only 30% of patients who got methadone without services lived abstinent.

Incentives may be effective way to incite abstinence from illicit drug utilization. In one field of study, 32% of methadone patients laid off all illicit drug use for prolonged periods of time when provided the opportunity to get methadone take-home privileges coming after drug-free urinalysis test results.

Only 8% of controls lay off drug use. Take-homes are the most potent reward available in the regular operation of methadone treatment plans.

In a different study with cocaine misusing methadone patients, the opportunity to obtain retail items from the program incited 47% of heavy cocaine substance abusers to quit using cocaine for lengthy periods of time during treatment. Only 6% of controls lay off utilizing cocaine for any meaningful length.

• **Treatment of Cocaine Substance Abusers**

Treatment of primary cocaine substance abusers relies totally on behavior and psychosocial therapies as there have been no effective medicines brought out to date.

Community Reinforcement therapy is a mighty new behavioral treatment for cocaine misuse. The treatment blends couples counseling, recreational therapy and physical incentives (retail items) that help to incite abstinence. The treatment holds patients in treatment (e.g. 58% retained for twenty-four weeks likened with 11% of controls) and boosts long durations of maintained abstinence.

Relapse prevention therapy, which instructs patients to realize high-risk situations for drug utilization and to go through coping techniques, has likewise demonstrated promise for treatment of cocaine substance abusers. Rates of retentiveness and abstinence have been better for relapse prevention than for control therapy in 2 studies.

## • Treatment of Tobacco Users

A lot of smokers who would like to quit prefer to do it on their own without any professional help. All the same, less than 10% of smokers who attempt to stop succeed on any given quit try (so attempt to stop 10 times and you ought to get it right once - that's a joke, but perhaps...)

Inquiry has identified particular physiological, psychological and environmental elements that lead to relapse versus successful abstinence after stopping.

Treatments may be tailored to address these components. Research has demonstrated that the most effective technique for smoking cessation blends nicotine replacement with patch or gum and behavior modification that teaches patients to realize high-risk situations for smoking and to carry out coping strategies. 30-40% may accomplish long-term abstinence with this plan of attack on a given quit attempt.

Smokers with a chronicle of depression have a particularly hard time stopping. Research has now demonstrated that these smokers may benefit from a particular mood management therapy in combination with nicotine replacement.

# Chapter 4- Other Equally Effective Drug Recovery Techniques

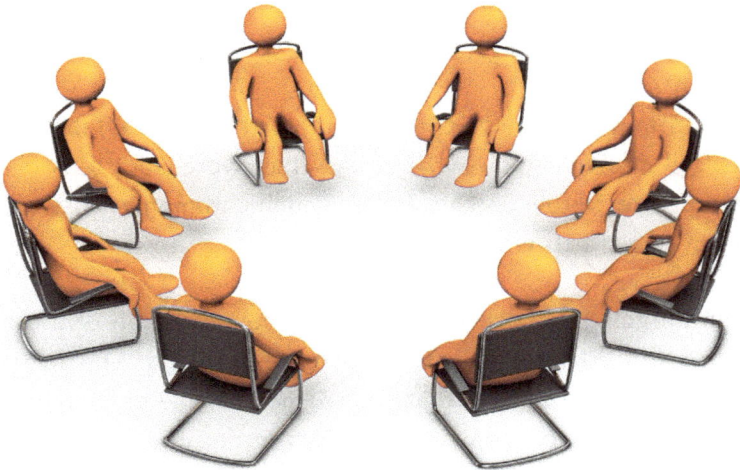

- **What is a Detox Clinic?**

Some addictions will require a person to go to a detox clinic before entering a rehab program. This is due to the fact that the withdrawals from the particular type of drug they have an addiction to can make them physically ill or even kill them. A common addiction that can lead to this is alcoholism. It is important to know the facts about detox and what a person may experience while going through a detox. It is highly advised that if possible you go to a detox center and don't try top detox on your own. It is best to be supervised by trained professionals in case and medical problems should occur.

It is important that I am honest with you about the topic of detox. It will not be an easy process. A person will likely experience many different side effects from their drug use. These side effects may be emotional, physical, or mental. A person will likely experience many uncomfortable feelings and not feel great about life during the process of detox but it is absolutely essential for recovery. After all, how will you ever begin your journey to recovery without first going over the speed bump of detox? The following are some examples of what a person may go through during detox:

**Sweats, Chills, Vomiting:**

A person may experience these uncomfortable side effects while detoxing, depending on what drugs they were addicted to. As stated before, heroin and alcohol addiction commonly cause these types of side effects when detoxing.

If you are going through this process at home instead of a clinic, which is not advised, you need to make sure that you hydrate yourself. Even if you know that you will not be able to keep liquids down you need to keep drinking. This is because you need to replace all the water you are losing from sweating and vomiting. Another reason it is advised to detox in a clinic is the fact that they can give you certain medications to help you feel better. A common drug prescribed to heroin abusers is methadone. You must be careful with methadone however because methadone can be addictive itself.

**Mood Changes:**

Detoxing from a drug can have great impact on a person's mood. A person who is usually happy, or seems to be because they are high, will be in a completely different mood. They may become irritable and snap at people for no reason or they may become depressed and think that life is no longer worth living. It is important to show understanding and compassion to a person who is going through this. Although it may be difficult to deal with their attitude, you can take pride in the fact that you know you are helping them with their problem. If you are the person going through the detox you should try your best not to take it out on others, but mood changes are expected.

**Cravings:**

Cravings are another one of the side effects of addiction. When a person is in the process of detoxing they will likely have very strong cravings. Some drugs may produce stronger cravings than others, so depending on the addiction a person has it might be a moderate craving or might be one that completely controls their thoughts momentarily. The trick to getting through this is to distract yourself when you feel a craving coming along. Talk with a friend or do a crossword. Anything that shifts the focus of your mind away from drugs will help. Although cravings feel like they will never go away, they do, and they actually get less often over time.

There are also of course positive outcomes from detoxing. The following are some examples:

**Better Health:**

Even though in the early stages of detox you might feel terrible, your health will actually already be starting to improve. You will notice the color coming back into your face and the dark circles leaving your eyes fairly quickly. You will feel more energetic and feel better than ever.

**Mental and Emotional State:**

You will notice that you begin thinking clearer and that things in reality begin to make more sense. This is because your mind is no longer being filled with the cloud of fog that addiction was causing.

As well, your emotional state will improve; you will be able to handle situations in life much better and more reasonably.

**Less Stress for Loved Ones:**

You loved ones will surely appreciate the fact that you have decided to get help and are now detoxing. This is sure to let sleep at night and no longer live in constant fear that they are going to lose you. Can you imagine how it must feel to have this concern for your child or other people you care for? It would be terrifying, wouldn't it?

**Better Self-Esteem:**

Beginning a detox process will surely boost your self-esteem. You will feel as if you can walk tall and hold your head up high once you are no longer being ruled by a substance. Not only will you be proud of yourself, those who are close to you will surely be proud of you to. It will feel much better during you next family get together or holidays when people know you are no longer using drugs and are in recovery. Their faces will surely be filled with joy and proudness instead of fear, concern, and disapproval.

● **The Importance of Rehab**

Drug rehabs are crucial to your recovery as they allow you to stride away from your life for a little while and center on merely becoming better. You won't have to fret about the everyday tensions of your life for a while and you are able to center all of your energy on merely coming through your drug dependency.

This is really helpful for many individuals as it lets them be able to view their lives from the exterior and there are occasionally matters that they're able to see about their lives while they're in treatment that they would not differently be able to see if they weren't in treatment.

Substance rehabs are likewise crucial to drug dependency recovery as they'll provide you the tools and the means to work out why you're addicted to substances first of all. You're going to be able to make batches of different decisions about why you turned to substances, and through these conclusions you're going to be able to work out what it was that made you need to become a substance addict or what guided to your drug dependency.

You'll be able to realize these matters in your life, so that when you're no longer in treatment and you have to contend with these same topics, you'll be able to make more beneficial decisions and ward off the traps that might lead to retrogressing into substance abuse.

Drug rehabs provide individuals the tools that they require to deal with the emotions that may commonly lead to substance abuse. If an addiction recovery individual may learn how to deal with tension, and emotions like rage and sorrow without utilizing drugs, then when they're in recovery and are confronted with these same emotions, they'll be better able to address them. It's really crucial that an individual becomes cognizant of different methods to deal with these emotions, as it's frequently these emotions that lead individuals back to drug abuse, even after recovery.

Drug rehabs are likewise going to bear services for loved ones and friends of individuals with substance addictions. There are going to be meetings that loved ones and friends may attend in which they'll hear all about what their loved one is experiencing, and they'll likewise learn ways to cope with their loved one and how to support them when they're in recovery. These meetings are really crucial to recovery, as it's frequently deficiency of support that leads somebody back to substance abuse.

Drug rehabs will likewise bear outpatient services that you yourself may go to while you're in recovery. These meetings and counseling sessions become really crucial in order to keep you clean and sober as they're places that will supply you with the support that you require.

**How to back-up Recovery**

Support yourself first of all – Support and love from loved ones and friends is a vital part of the recovery process. Support for the loved ones and friends of the recovering addict are of like importance. That's why addiction groups have developed – to help outsiders comprehend the addiction and how best to back up the recovery process. It's crucial for them to comprehend that they're not at fault for their acquaintance or loved ones addiction.

Step in – frequently, the support of friends and loved ones is most required during the beginning step of the recovery stage – admitting there's an issue and seeking professional help. This may take the form of an intervention, where friends and loved ones get together to present a unified presence of love and concern for the addict in a non-confrontational fashion. This procedure may likewise take the form of appealing from loved ones or even ultimatums if the state of affairs gets bad enough.

Prepare – Read everything you are able to on addiction and the recovery process. This will advance your understanding of what the patient is going through in detox, counseling and treatment. It will likewise help you comprehend best how to offer support during the aftercare stage, after release from the recovery treatment center.

Don't label, don't enable – Never quit expressing your trust in the patient's power to recover from an addiction. At the same time, be steadfast and let them understand you care enough to hold them accountable. You are able to do this in a non-judgmental, loving fashion. Abstain from substance use and from bringing up substances in conversation.

Think about attending religious services together or becoming involved in a voluntary service project or community education class. While remaining busy is a great distraction, attempt not to overdo it, as the patient will still be working on a lot mentally and emotionally during aftercare.

- **Hypnosis**

When an individual takes any substance, the chemistry of his or her body will alter. For instance, if you have a head ache and you consume an aspirin, commonly the infliction will disappear, and if you consume recreational drugs, they'll commonly bring about a feeling of euphoria.

After the personal effects of a substance wear away, the user might be enticed to consume more of it to go through the same effect once more, even if they had a head ache and it has not reoccurred. When you truly like the effects of either recreational or prescription medicine, then you might potentially become drug-addicted and hooked on them.

Individuals who become addicted will commonly decide to stop their drug dependence when they recognize the negative outcomes the drug is having on their life story. Drugs might greatly impact them physically and hide their real personality, commonly this is what is seen with tranquilizer and antidepressant drug use. There are likewise a lot of damaging side effects like fatigue that might be experienced by those who attempt to kick their substance abuse habit.

If you've been utilizing recreational drugs on a steady basis, always remember to confer with a physician before you attempt to quit taking them. For your own safety, drug withdrawal from substances need to be supervised medically in most cases. Physicians may likewise provide you a support network that may help in you in your fight.

Hypnotherapy may assist those of you who don't wish to consume recreational drugs any longer, but most times it's safer to look for professional hypnotherapists who specialize in that field.

Ask a professional hypnotherapy association to discover their members who have been schooled to deal with your own specific state of affairs. As you discover the correct hypnotherapist, talk to him about your fears regarding the treatment, he will assess your needs and deal with the resolution of problems that induced your addiction. He will likewise help you boost up your self-respect and build up your strength as you go through the treatment.

Make sure that when you're addicted to recreational substances, you always ask your physician's guidance first before you undergo hypnotherapy. Bringing the use of prescription medicine or illicit drugs to an end isn't simple; it has to be executed slowly to let the body recuperate the chemicals that have been replaced by the substance.

Through hypnotherapy, the elements that sparked your drug dependency will be distinguished and dealt with. Self-hypnosis can likewise support you in accomplishing your desired outcome.

Hypnotherapy put together with additional treatments needs your full dedication to succeed but they might well help you come through the transition more easily once you've determined to quit taking drugs.

- **The Power of Self-Suggestions**

**Design**

In order to be successful at utilizing affirmations you have to have a clear-cut step by step game design. You have to set a time aside where you are able to utter your affirmations aloud every single day for at the least one calendar month.

It's most beneficial to write your affirmations down first of all and then as you learn them you are able to narrate them in your own words. If you are able to state your affirmations aloud each day for more than 21 days, you'll discover this to be unbelievably powerful.

**Get Moving**

State aloud so you are able to hear your own voice the accompanying:

"I understand that I have got the power to quit drugs today. Consequently I require of myself doggedness and ceaseless action towards the goal of laying off drugs now. I'm creating a promise to myself that I can and will stop"

We today know that through the precept of affirmation and suggestion that the recurrent act of stating desire toward your goal will sooner or later become physical truth. Consequently it's advised that you spend equal to 30 minutes each and every single day, and spend that time on considering the drug free individual you intend to turn into. As you affirm your target of quitting drugs, make a clear-cut mental image of this individual you're turning into.

As you rehearse this you'll discover it works in a predictable style. As you continually and repeatedly bear in your mind the picture of your fresh self, you'll discover that you slowly and mechanically transform your truth in positive ways. Consequently it's crucial to spend 10 minutes of every day, requiring of yourself the self-control and self-assurance to quit drugs.

**Devote**

In order to devote yourself even more to this procedure, make sure to get it down in writing. Put down a description of your goal to stop drugs and promise to never quit trying, till you've developed the self-control to stop. It will be something you are able to go back to.

**Reward**

In conclusion, you'll wish to remind yourself every day about some of the basic principles of affirmation. Simply recall that affirmations will carry on working for you as long as you only utilize them in fashions that benefit yourself and everybody around you.

You'll sooner or later pull in to yourself the outcomes, places, and things you'll need to utilize, likewise the cooperation of others. Remember to formulate within yourself a love for all individuals, and particularly love for yourself. You'll discover that individuals are more than willing to assist you, as you're the type of individual who's helpful towards other people.

Carry with you your personal statement of affirmation at all times, and put your name to it. Make certain to commit it to memory and recite it aloud each day.

Utilize your faith and your emotions, and you'll discover that you step by step influence your own actions, quit abusing drugs, and become and successful and self-governing individual. Remember the steps for affirmation, provide you the most beneficial suggestions for quitting drugs, and make that a habit.

You'll discover that you by nature produce a plan for quitting and follow that plan by utilizing affirmation and self-suggestion.

# Chapter 5- Discussing Drugs with a Minor

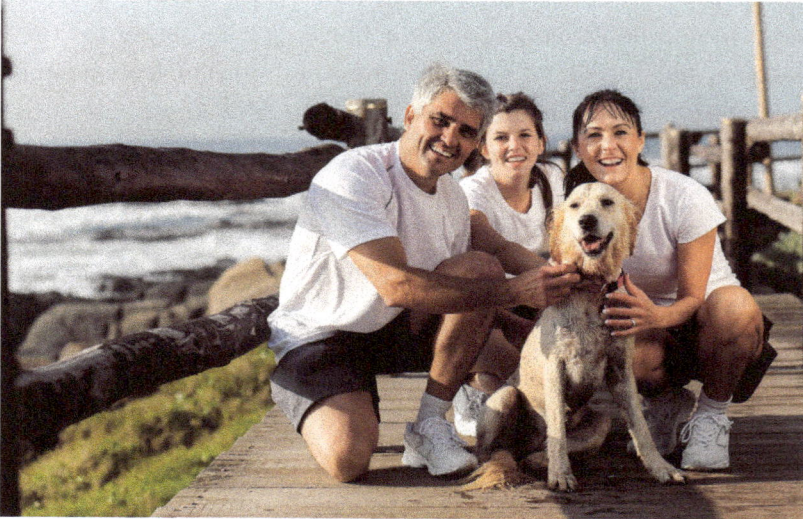

Talking about drugs is a sensitive topic. That is the reason why you should pick the right time and have the right attitude when discussing about it. But, when is the right time and how to know if you have the right attitude to discuss drugs?

Since talking about drugs is not the same as talking about the activities at school, you should always know the right time and have the right attitude for you to discuss successfully. There are several ways on how to know the right time and having the right attitude. Some of these are as follows:

• **Know Your Kid's Schedule**

Knowing your children's schedule is important if you want to pick the right time and have the right attitude. If your kids are busy with their school activities, don't interrupt them. The reason behind it is that they might not concentrate on what you are saying and could think of something that would allow them to accomplish their school activities. If possible, know your kid's free time or you could inform them in advance that you want to talk about something important so they could allot time for you.

## • Bond with Your Children First

Bonding with your children first could let you set their mind and can allow you to pick the right time easily. Plus, you could quickly have the right attitude as you are all having fun with your bonding. But, when discussing about drugs, don't give them shocking introduction. Try to take it slowly but in a serious manner.

## • Make Sure to Discuss During Your Free Time

Your free time is always the right time for you to discuss about drugs. Just make sure to focus on the discussion and turn off your devices so that if anyone calls you, you will not get distracted. However, even if it is your free time, make sure that it's the free time of your children too. Through this, you and your children could focus and take the topic seriously.

## • Take Away Everything That May Disturb Your Discussion with Your Children

Taking away everything that may disturb your discussion with your children will let them focus on what you say. If your kids are watching TV or playing games with their game consoles, you can tell them to turn it off first for you to have some talk with them.

Considering those mentioned details above will not just let you achieve success, but also you can guarantee that your kids have understood everything you have discussed. So, always pick the right time and have the right attitude.

**Creativity Works Wonders**

Some surveys showed that there are kids who are not comfortable talking to their parents about what they feel and what they are going through. These are also those who aren't comfortable talking about how to stay free from drugs as well as excessive use of alcohol.

**•Give Information Appropriate for Their Age**

Simple details repeated on important occasions must get the message across regarding the dangers of alcohol and drugs. For instance, if your kid is eating fruits, you can talk with them regarding how fruits are good and healthy for their body.

When it comes to drugs, if these are exposed in conversations or media, you can ask your kid if they know what this means. Tell them that those are addictive and could harm one's bodies severely. If they ask some details, don't hesitate to answer them.

The older your kids get, the more information they would seek. Make sure that you are updated with the drug names and how they could affect one's body so that you could give the right details. If you don't know all the answers, there are more facts you will find.

• **Indicate Your Family Values**

Your children should know how you feel about using drugs and consuming alcohol. For instance, you could say that in your family, you don't agree taking any kind of drugs unless your doctor says so.

It's quite dangerous to provide this on your own as this is a serious stuff. Several individuals have made mistakes in taking numerous drugs and they became sick and some already died.

• **Tell Them about Your Beliefs**

Show your children that you always practice what you preach. Avoid drinking alcohol excessively if you want your kids to be responsible drinkers. If you are taking tons of vitamins, try doing it discreetly.

• **Talk about Peer Pressure**

Your kids need to determine good friends from bad one. Good friends are always there to care and listen to them. People trying to pressure them into drinking, smoking or using drugs are not good friends. Encourage your children to engage in different healthy activities like sports to be fit, feel good, and be energetic.

There are other ways you could explain the risks of drugs. Depending on what you believe in, you can explain that sometimes adults enjoy a glass of alcohol. Tell them that when alcohol is consumed too often, this would be the time that it is dangerous.

You should pick the right time to talk about drugs to your kids. Children are being exposed with various things like alcohol and drugs. Start encouraging them how they could take care of themselves as well as take pride in their healthy bodies.

If you don't know everything about drugs, there is nothing you should worry about as you can consider making a research. There are lots of resources available out there. However, make sure that they are accurate and would help you guide your children. If you don't know where to get started, asking help from experts can offer you a big hand.

## What Happens When You Ignore Your Child's Addiction?

Some parents are too confident about their children's behaviors. They think that their children are wise and knowledgeable enough when it comes to drugs. But, did you know that even if your kid is the best in class, there's a possibility that he or she could abuse or be addicted to drugs? Well, this happens especially if you don't consider drug talk in your home. If you are a parent, you should pay importance to drug talk as there are dangers in not having this kind of conversation. So, what are these dangers?

Drug talk is said to be one of the best ways for you, as a parent, to educate and guide your children about drugs. Even if you always have a busy schedule, don't take drugs for granted as you might end up facing a complicated situation that you might regret for the rest of your life. Though your schedule is hectic, you will always have your spare time. Instead of doing some activities at home, why not sit and talk to your children about their daily activities and let them know about the risks of taking drugs?

There are several dangers in not having a drug talk. One of these is that your kids might seek for answers with their friends who are already using drugs. In this scenario, your kids could also end up using drugs, which might ruin their future or worst – their lives. Since they don't have any clue about drugs and some of their friends said that they should try it once to know the effects, they could abuse and get addicted to the substance they are taking especially if the effects are good and they don't see anything bad about it.

Most children are curious about almost everything even with drugs. More often than not, there are instances that some kids would try using drugs to test if these are really bad and could ruin their lives. If they don't see anything negative about drugs, they would continue use these until they end up abusing these, which could be dangerous in the long run.

There are other dangers of not having a drug talk. If you want your kids to stay on the right direction, do not waste your time and start talking with them about drugs because there is always a difference in having a drug talk and not having it.

# CHAPTER 6- THE JOYS OF BEING DRUG AND ALCOHOL FREE

For many individuals, getting off drugs and alcohol isn't the hardest part of getting rid of addiction. Living drug and alcohol free is the most challenging part. There are tons of reasons for this. One of these is some feeling of pain when fleeing. This pain can be the cause of abandonment, child abuse, being a gay or lesbian or loss of a loved one. There are not easy problems, but this can much harder if combined with the problem of recovering from drugs and alcohol.

No matter what your reasons why you started using drugs or alcohol, you should try your best to be alcohol and drug free. Once you stop using drugs or alcohol, you will be able to experience numerous advantages which you haven't thought of.

Living in a drug-free life can provide more freedom compared to the artificial feeling of freedom you can get from being high. Drug users may try escaping through addiction. They may be stressful after work and use drugs to relax. Addiction doesn't provide a solution or healing. It can't also provide the benefits of living in a drug-free life, which may include the following:

**Family**

One of the most essential aspects in living a drug-free life is the family aspect. Drug addiction or abuse could tear families apart. Drug use may cause mood swings, violence, cheating, financial troubles, and lying. There are no numerous families that may remain standing during drug addiction, yet a drug-free life can let families heal.

**Stress Management**

Even if tons of people feel as if drugs take away stress, addiction and abuse do exactly the opposite. Once someone became dependent upon any drugs, just the thought of aren't being able to take another can be stressful. Between trying to seek more drugs, hiding drug use from your loved ones and financial stress can be overbearing. No matter where you live, being drug-free can be less stressful.

**Career**

Living in a drug-free life will let you excel and keep your job. Some drug users find it hard to concentrate or care about their job. In addition to that, addiction could also get you fired. You aren't only harming yourself, but also other people that surround you.

**Mental Stability**

Tons of drugs can cause mental health problems and these may often lead to addiction in drugs. Once this starts, this will require professional help and hard work to stop. Searching for a drug-free life may provide you much required mental stability.

**Wellbeing**

Your overall wellbeing is at stake once you abused any drug. This may include your friendships, values and priorities, physical health, and family. Living in a drug-free life can benefit you in each aspect of your life.

There are other benefits you could acquire from being drug-free. If you don't want to ruin your life and every aspect of your life, then don't hesitate to get rid of drugs and start stopping taking these. There are other things that you could do with your life. You don't need drugs to get rid of your issues or personal problems. Drugs are not solutions. These will just give you a relief for the meantime, but in the long run, this will start ruining your life.

**It's Possible to Live Life without Alcohol**

For some, not consuming alcohol could be a difficult task. Though alcohol isn't really prohibited for people who are 21 years and above, it is always wise to drink moderately as addiction in alcohol could be dangerous and might ruin everything you have already achieved.

Not drinking alcohol could offer you healthy bodies and cheerful minds. You will not deal with hangovers and DUIs. Getting off your habit will assist you in maintaining a positive outlook, useful decisions, and live in a better life. Your work will improve. Your relationship and mind-set will improve including those with your own family. Overall, not drinking alcohol could benefit you in various ways. Below are some of them:

**Healthier Liver**

One of the numerous functions of one's liver is the alcohol's assimilation. Majority of alcohol that you consume is absorbed and metabolized into the body through liver. This body organ can only process half ounce of alcohol each hour. If you have consumed more, the liver can't process this and complications could arise in your vital systems because of the reason that your blood will have high content of alcohol. Moreover, if this goes unchecked for a period of time, your liver can be damaged permanently. You will also suffer from other liver disorders that are caused by alcohol.

Getting rid of alcohol can offer you a healthier liver, which is a vital organ. Without this, no one will ever survive.

**Sharper Brain**

Because of alcohol, brain cells can be affected. Using too much of alcohol could result to lesions on one's brain. This can also damage the cognitive functions as well as memory. Those who are addicted to alcohol can sometimes lose one's ability to form long-term memory. Because of the alcohol's inhibition-lowering effect, this has been linked with the increased domestic violence, child abuse, and teenage pregnancies. On the other hand, teetotalers may always maintain a grasp over themselves as well as be responsible for actions.

**Sound Heart**

Even if moderate wine consumption is renowned for reducing the risks of various heart ailments, majority of the alcoholic beverages have alcohol compared to wine and this may contribute to the HDL buildup instead of preventing it. That is the reason why if you don't want your heart to get damaged by alcohol, then live in an alcohol-free life.

**Improved Sex Life**

Prolonged alcohol abuse may cause hormonal imbalance in the body. This could result in the estrogen's hyper secretion that can lead to impotence of men and sexual dysfunction. Not consuming alcohol could provide anyone with stable hormone levels.

**Lesser Risk of Cancer**

Hormonal imbalance that caused impotence in men may lead to breast cancer to women. Alcohol is also been linked with different ailments of pancreas like the pancreatic cancer.

**Safer Pregnancies**

Placental barrier between the mother and her baby is permeable to the alcohol. If the alcohol is consumed by the pregnant woman, the fetus can be invariably affected. This can lead to miscarriage, severe congenital disorder or stillbirth in the baby. Even though you're not a teetotaler, alcohol must not be drunk when they are pregnant. Putting down alcohol can put you at lesser risk when you are pregnant so you can avoid medical complications.

**Avoid Obesity**

Alcohol may contain more sugar compared to fruits, yet no nutrients. This can lead to unhealthy weight gain. Obesity increases the chances of having a more serious problem like heart problems, diabetes, depression, and many more. This is very hard to minimize weight gained because of alcohol. During that time, one has realized this, but it is typically too late.

**Better Sleep**

Even though alcohol is depressants and cause drowsiness, this disturbs sleep patterns particularly in your sleep's second half. You have to take not that having a better sleep could let you do more and be more productive, which can be beneficial in your career especially if you have busy schedules.

**Improved Social Life**

Alcohol addiction could also cause social and psychological problems. As mentioned earlier, alcohol can cause hormonal imbalance in one's body, which can cause frequent insomnia, depression, dementia, and so on. Even though alcoholic beverages are also part of fabric of numerous cultures, alcohol's abusive overuse is often condemned through societal norms, which can lead to alcoholic becoming outcast. If you will not consume alcohol, you will be able to get rid of mental or psychological problems that could allow you to live in a more improved social life. If being drug and alcohol free is a hard thing to do, there is nothing you should worry about. The reason behind it is that you can rely on professionals who could provide you some services designed to make your life much better. However, make sure to take it slowly. Don't force yourself too much to avoid any inconvenience. Once you have successfully gotten rid of drug and alcohol, you will be able to enjoy all those mentioned benefits above.

# CHAPTER 7- PARENTS AS GOOD ROLE MODELS

There is no such thing as being a perfect parent. Parents have the hardest jobs in the world. It's a special joy to raise kids, but this can be demanding, exhausting, and challenging. Plus, there is no day off. Each parent has bad days and good days. Yet, each day, you serve as a role model for your children.

You have to take note that your child learns from what you say and what you do. Your child also thinks the same way like you do as well as copies your expressions. Before your kids go to school, they have also probably learned even more from than you ever wanted.

**Is It Something You Should Worry About?**

Your kid will grow up as well as have to make choices for grown-up. If you show restraint in terms of alcohol, gambling, and drugs, then there is a huge possibility that your kids will follow your example. If you're considerate to others and you control your temper, you child will likely copy your behavior.

**Are Other People Role Models for Your Child?**

Friends, uncles, aunts or grandparents that spend time with your kids are role models. A coach, teacher or neighbor may also be a role model.

Having an adult who cares can make a huge difference. Even when there is conflict or life is tough, if an individual supports and cares a child, this can also make a difference. If there's someone to stand by your kid no matter what, your kids will be able to get over the tough times.

Anyone may be a role model, yet main caregivers or parents have the most influence on the child. Even if your child is now a teen and does not seem interested in you, she or he is watching you as the role model.

**How to be a Good Role Model?**

Consider how your behavior affects your children. This is not likely that you may always be cheerful and calm. Well, no one is. Children need to see parents express real feeling in a healthy manner. If your kid has witnessed that you are dealing with your anger appropriately, she or he will learn this from you. If he or she watches you celebrating special occasions without taking alcohol, your kid will learn something. If you are facing a hard time and you are trying to escape it with drugs, gambling, and alcohol, your kid will remember it. Therefore, as your kid grows up, she or he will learn by your example. Your kid will also follow your example when coping with the challenges.

**What If You Make Mistakes That You Don't Want Your Kid to Copy?**

If you have problems in your family, even your kid can be affected. In most cases, children believe that they are the cause of the problem or they did something wrong.

You can assist your children by talking with them. Even young kids could understand your sincere apology. It is possible to be honest with your kid. You can say sorry and explain mistakes, yet you are doing your best to change. You should also tell your child that you love her or him that problems are not her or his fault.

**How Can You Teach Your Child about Some Positive Role Models?**

Talking to your child regarding the things that could happened to you when you are her or his age. Tell your children about someone who made a huge difference in your life and tell them the reasons. This could someone you know.

Understanding the different individuals behave in various ways could help your child. Your kid could start thinking about who makes a role model.

No one said that it is easy to be a role model. But, it is not impossible that you can do it especially if it is for your child's sake.

# Chapter 8- The Importance of Support Groups and Follow-up Programs

Support groups and follow up programs can be quite useful in the battle for your life with addiction. There are numerous support groups out there for every type of addiction including drugs, sex, food, self-harm, video games, porn and many others. Support groups and follow up programs can be located online or through local outreach programs. If you have never tried a support group it is worth a shot. You will likely be surprised by how much a support group can help you.

Support groups and follow up programs can be very beneficial for your battle against addiction. Support groups provide a setting for open discussion about the difficulties related to addiction and recovery. Most support groups will encourage you to have a sponsor. A sponsor is your guide while working towards recovery. You should choose a sponsor who has been drug-free for at least one year. You want them to be experienced when it comes to recovery so they can offer you proper guidance. Your sponsor will also help you work on your steps if your support group participates in a twelve step program. A couple support groups that use the 12 steps are AA and NA.

If you choose to go to a support group like AA or NA you will be provided with rewards for your accomplishment of being drug-free. Your reward is being given a chip which represents the number of days you have clean. They present you with this reward in front of the whole group. This boosts your self-esteem and also encourages others in the group to continue with their treatment. It shows people that it is possible and that you do not have to be super human in order to win the battle against addiction.

It is also very helpful to hear other people's stories of their battle with addiction and the challenges they had to overcome. Most people have the error of thinking their life is worse than everyone else's. Support groups provide people with an opportunity to hear stories of situations and losses that are much worse than theirs.

The fact that you are part of a group will also be a motivator for you during your battle. You can think of it as being part of a team and your team's objective is to remain drug free and beat the battle of addiction. Each person who stays clean contributes to the team's strength while those who are falling behind receive help and encouragement from the stronger team members. Eventually everyone in the team is strong until a new person enters the team. The same process takes place over again until everyone on the team is strong once again.

Another advantage of support groups is the fact that they are cost-free. This eliminates using money as any sort of excuse to not go. You can receive help and advice that some people may consider to be more valuable than advice provided by a counselor for free from a support group, so why not give it a try, what could it hurt?

# Chapter 9- Proper Nutrition for Recovery

A large part of winning in your battle with addiction is to have a proper diet. This may be hard to believe but it is true. While a person is trying to gain control of their addiction it is essential that they have a well-balanced diet and avoid certain things like excessive sugar and caffeine. It is advised to look over the food pyramid while constructing a diet.

It is important while in recovery to have a proper diet. This will make you feel good, and when you feel good you will have less of a need to use drugs to feel good. As well, drug-abuse caused by addiction takes a serious toll on the health of a person's body. Therefore, you should eat properly to start regaining your strength and good health.

Studies have been conducted that show that certain diets can help an addict with their recovery. These studies state that the daily diet of a recovering addict should include:

30% Fat

25% Protein

45% Carbohydrates

You may find yourself asking, what type of meals will be consistent with that daily diet? A few examples include:

**Breakfast:**

Try eating some pancakes with an egg omelet and some yogurt on the side. An oatmeal muffin is also another great idea.

**Lunch:**

Sandwiches are a great source of carbohydrates because of the bread and protein because of the meat (if you put meat on your sandwich.)

**Dinner:**

For dinner you may try eating chowder or some rice and beans. Chicken and vegetables is also another good idea. Lasagna can even be a great healthy dinner.

**Dessert:**

For dessert you can have some yogurt or some custard. You might also want to try eating a piece of fruit or some oatmeal cookies.

It is important to remember that like anything else, these things are only good in moderation. For example, you may see fruit as healthy, but fruit is packed with sugar, so even too much fruit can be a bad thing. As well, just because chicken is healthy does not mean you can have an entire chicken for dinner. Remember, everything in moderation.

It is important to avoid excessive amounts of sugar and caffeine. The reason for this is the fact that they are stimulants. They can slightly mimic the effect of certain drugs which may cause triggers in some people.

If you are a smoker, another part of your diet geared towards recovery should be to quit smoking. Many people are unaware of the fact that nicotine is in fact a stimulant. So just like caffeine, it can cause triggers. Also, the smoke might remind a person of using a certain type of drug and make them have a craving.

# About The Author

Rachel Chloe Sanchez is a social worker working with recovery addicts. She has been helping addicts find their way back to drug-free lives and be accepted by their families again for over 15 years.

Rachel, herself, was once addicted to alcohol. She struggled for two years following her divorce and the death of her child. She thought her life was over and drowned herself in misery and alcohol. She was in a state of despair that her parents found her and helped her.

Today, Rachel has been alcohol-free for over 20 years. She has re-married and has a son serving in the navy.

Lightning Source UK Ltd.
Milton Keynes UK
UKHW020956250522
403474UK00006B/96